Ban This Book!

Ban This Book!

a cartoon collection by
Pat Oliphant

Foreword by Larry L. King

Andrews and McMeel, Inc.
A Universal Press Syndicate Company
Kansas City • New York

ISBN: 0-8362-1251-7
Library of Congress Catalog Card Number: 82-72414

For Studs Terkel

Foreword to the Foreword

Studs Terkel should be writing this. But for one thing, he's gone to Russia. For two, there's a deadline involved. Three, when Larry L. King heard that someone else would do the foreword for this year's collection, he stopped drinking and refused to speak to anyone for three days. So Studs has promised to do it next year, and in recognition of the fact that he has indeed had a real live book banned this year, I think I'll dedicate this collection to him. This will disturb King, but not mortally. So here for the third time is Laurence L. King with more fulminations on my habits public and private. He is forbidden the use of the word "curmudgeon."

A Hasty Tribute to Dr. Oliphant

This is the third consecutive time I have been asked to write the foreword to Pat Oliphant's collected cartoon offerings.

The honor is limited by certain circumstances.

Three Oliphant books ago I was the first, and only, writer he asked to perform the flattering task. No deadline pressures then existed. I leisurely researched Pat's life and work, brutally telling the truth in each instance.

Indeed, I so flawlessly introduced *Oliphant!* that he almost desperately sought another writer to introduce *The Jellybean Society* a year later. I think he also had his head turned by Dartmouth University, which, between books, had made him an honorary Doctor of Humane Letters — probably as some lame campus joke — so that Dr. Oliphant wished his newest Art to be presented by someone who had written something a mite classier than *The Best Little Whorehouse in Texas.*

But, alas, because the other scribes wouldn't work for five dollars and claimed writer's block, Dr. Oliphant approached me at the eleventh hour, begging and whining that I present him anew. I did so, again hewing hard to the truth, revealing how he is a rather grouchy old sod who mistreats dogs and eschews children. While Dr. Oliphant's limited friends almost to the last in number huzzahed my accurate prose, the learned Doctor himself was less than charitable in his critique.

"Wait till next year," he threatened.

Try as I might to avoid the churlish old fellow, I kept bumping into him for lunch about three times weekly. At each of our bread-breakings Dr. Oliphant would offer the names of superior writers clamoring to write in the space I am filling now.

"Norman Mailer," he would say with a smug smirk. "William Styron. Jimmy Breslin. Kurt Vonnegut. That foreign fella who writes all that deep stuff I don't understand — oh, you know, that Russian that was always bitching about Russia until he came here and switched sides."

"Solzhenitsyn," I instructed him.

"Naw, naw," the learned Doctor said. "Ain't he a hockey player?"

Anyhow, for one reason and another, Dr. Oliphant was unable to land all those superior writers. At lunch today he threw himself slobbering at my feet and cried his woes: "Studs Terkel was gonna do it but he didn't answer my calls for six months. When I reached him, he claimed to be on the way to China or Wyoming and didn't have time. Ann Landers is too busy typing old letters to be recycled in her column. For a while there I thought I had Mrs. Rutherford B. Hayes, but somebody said she died. Hell, I didn't even know she was sick."

"Okay, Dr. Oliphant," I said. "Gimme the five dollars."

He did, almost pathetically thanking me for again getting his ox out of the ditch, and licking my hand.

I would have preferred to have seen the cartoons before writing this cheery and uplifting foreword to *Ban This Book!* but Dr. Oliphant was in such a time bind he allowed as how I must write this tribute totally in the blind. That being the case, I particularly recommend those cartoons on pages 89 and 126.

Working without specifics, I must now fall back on history and generalities by telling you that Dr. Oliphant has, on slow days in the business, won the Pulitzer Prize, the Sigma Delta Chi Award, the Reuben Award from the American Cartoonist Society no less than four times, and the National Headliner Award for editorial cartooning once or twice. The last I heard none of these baubles had been recalled.

So it is a great honor to once again present Dr. Oliphant's latest collection, though I may have been his 139th choice.

I look on the bright side: How many Americans have managed to hang on to their jobs for three consecutive years during the Reagan administration?

And as for you, Dr. Oliphant: Wait till next year.

—Larry L. King
Designated Pinch Hitter

Afterword

Mr. King, who normally has all the suave poise of Popeye, is becoming more testy with age and may not be invited to perform this small service for many years more. I do expect he may next start clamoring for tenure and billing on the cover.

All this may be moot, however, as Mr. King's well-publicized feud with one Mr. Reynolds, a star of the silver screen, has progressed to the point where that enraged gentleman has volunteered to tear off one of Mr. King's arms and beat him to death with it.

Whatever happened to manners? . . .

— Pat Oliphant

July 16, 1981

OLIPHANT
WHAT??
NO, SIR—
WATT!!
WELCOME TO
CALIFORNIA
OFF-SHORE
DRILLING

July 21, 1981

'ALL VERY FINE FOR YOU. WHEN I GO ON STRIKE, PEOPLE WON'T EVEN NOTICE FOR THE FIRST THREE WEEKS.'

July 22, 1981

July 23, 1981

'OH, OH, EVE — IT'S THAT CREATIONIST NUT, JERRY FALWELL AGAIN!'

July 28, 1981

'CAN'T YOU STOP HOUNDING ME TILL I GET CLEANED UP?'

July 28, 1981

BUT, CHARLES, WHAT'S TO BE DONE ABOUT THE NATION'S AWFUL ECONOMIC STATE? ABOUT ALL THE UNEMPLOYED? AND ALL THE DREADFUL RIOTING? AND ABOUT THE HUNGER STRIKES...?
DON'T BE TIRESOME, DEAR...
THEY SAY THEY'VE GOT EVERYTHING THEY WANT, MA'AM
OLIPHANT

July 30, 1981

'DEAR PRESIDENT REAGAN; IS THERE A FOOD-FOR-PEACE LOAN FOR SOCIAL SECURITY RETIREES..?'

July 31, 1981

I DUCK!
I WEAVE!
I GOTTIM ON DA ROPES
A LEFT TO DA BODY
A RIGHT TO DA JAW
KID O'NEILL
WRIGHT GYM
WRIGHTS GYM
DA FANS IS SCREAMIN'
OLIPHANT

August 3, 1981

'YOU'RE ON WHAT?'

August 4, 1981

THE HOSTAGES OF AYATOLLAH POLI

August 7, 1981

'AH, THE BEAUTIFUL, CLEAN, FRESH AIR... PITY THERE'S NOT ENOUGH FOR EVERYONE.'

August 10, 1981

'THANK YOU, DR. WEINBERGER. I THINK WE'LL CALL HIM NEUTRON.'

August 12, 1981

August 18, 1981

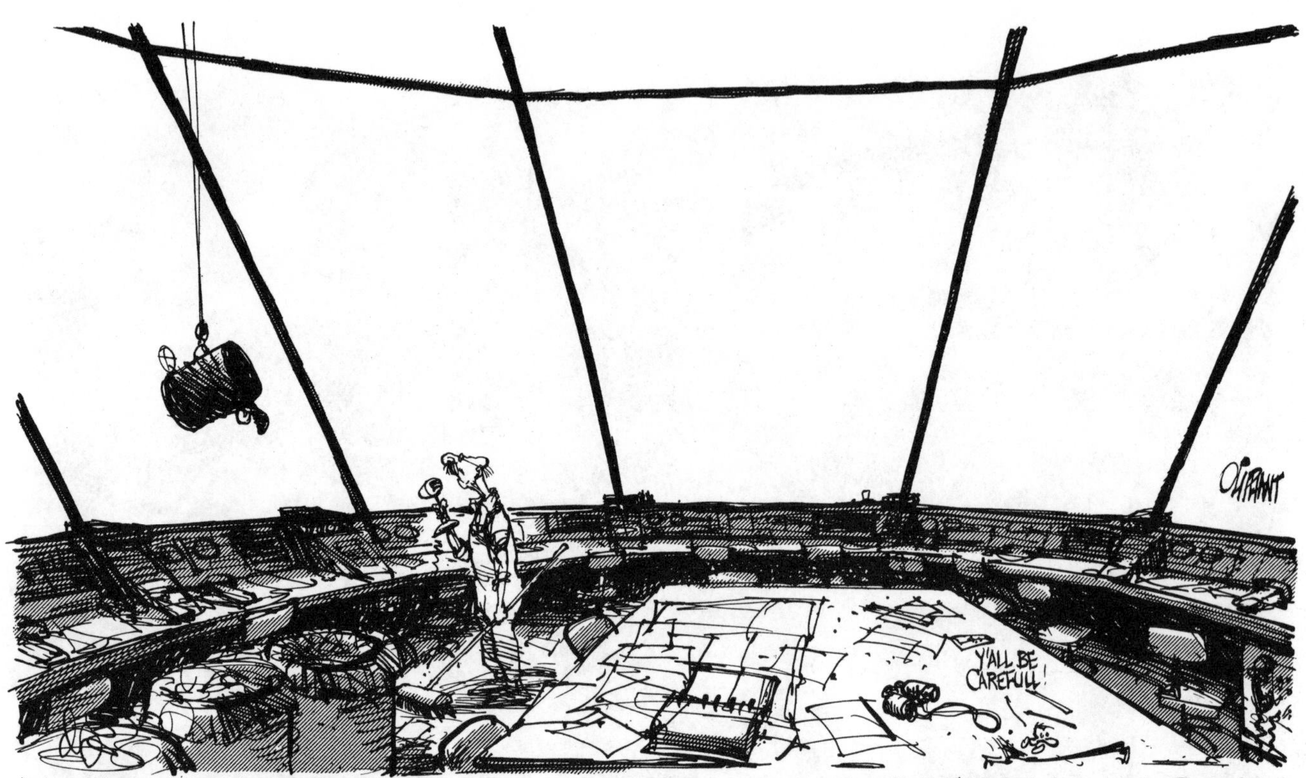

'ONE THREE KILO CLEARED FOR TAKEOFF RUNWAY NINER ZERO, NINER FOUR FOXTROT TAXI TO POSITION AND HOLD, OSCAR CHARLIE MAKE A STRAIGHT IN APPROACH ON ONE SIX LEFT...'

August 20, 1981

THE BROWN BOMBER

August 21, 1981

August 24, 1981

'I'LL SLEEP ON IT. WHEN YOU GUYS HAVE FIGURED IT OUT, WAIT SIX HOURS, THEN SURPRISE ME.'

August 25, 1981

August 27, 1981

'YUP, PATCO'S STILL ON STRIKE AND THE POSTAL WORKERS AIN'T. NORTH KOREA TOSSED A MISSILE AT A U.S. PLANE. THE MEDFLIES ARE GITTIN' WORSE AND INTEREST RATES... HEY, YOU GONE TO SLEEP AGIN, BOY?'

August 31, 1981

'KAPOW! JUST LISTEN TO THAT FIRING SQUAD! LONG LIVE THE REVOLUTION!'

September 1, 1981

HARD TIMES AT THE PENTAGON, PART ONE: TAKING UP A COLLECTION TO BUY ANOTHER CANNONBALL.

September 2, 1981

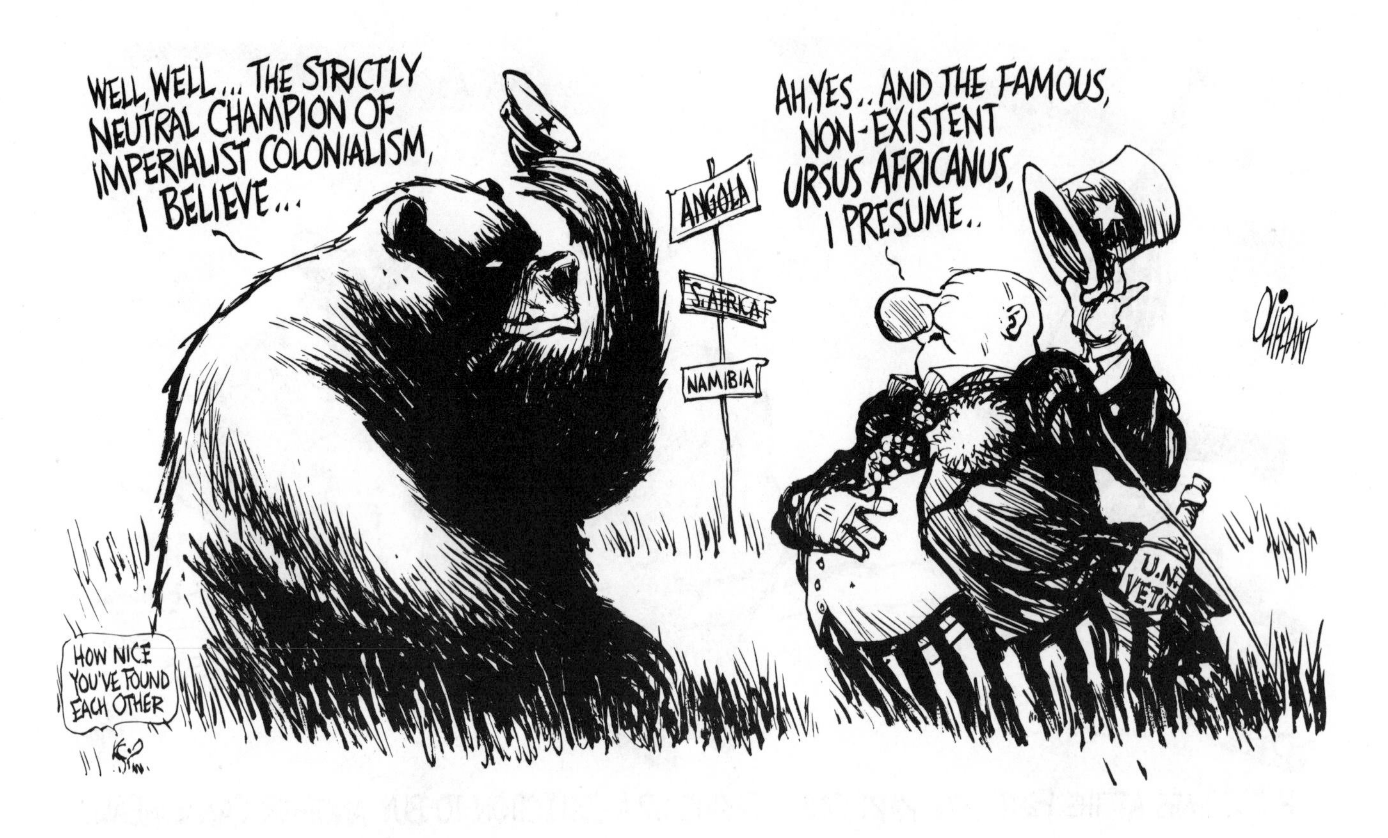

September 4, 1981

'WE AGREED TO TAKE HIS PAPERS, AND WE BUILT HIS LIBRARY. BUT WE COMPROMISED ON THE NAME.'

September 8, 1981

'HEY, WHY DON'T YOU ALL TAKE A MONTH OFF? — I CAN RECOMMEND IT.'

September 10, 1981

'OK, WATT— HOLD IT RIGHT THERE!'

September 10, 1981

'SANDRA O'CONNOR, HOW PLEAD YOU TO THE HEINOUS CHARGE OF SECULAR WOMANISM?'

September 11, 1981

September 14, 1981

'OH, REALLY? WHAT PATTERN?'

September 15, 1981

'AMAZING — AND THE MIRROR COMES WITH IT, RIGHT?'

September 16, 1981

'SORRY, SIR. WE'VE BEEN HAVING A FEW ALCOHOL AND DRUG RELATED PROBLEMS ABOARD, SIR!'

September 17, 1981

'WE BETTER STOP GIVING PASS-FAIL GRADES. THE JAPANESE ENGINE SURVIVED, BUT THE REST OF THE CAR'S A WIPE-OUT.'

September 18, 1981

September 21, 1981

September 23, 1981

September 25, 1981

'UP!'

September 28, 1981

'NOW THAT STOCKMAN HAS RE-APPROVED VEGETABLES FOR THE SCHOOL LUNCH, WE'D BETTER GET SOME HAY IN FOR THE WINTER.'

A WESTERNER'S VIEW OF AN EASTERNER'S VIEW OF THE UNITED STATES.

October 2, 1981

'BUSINESS WAS NEVER BETTER!'

October 6, 1981

October 7, 1981

ROAD TO NOWHERE

October 9, 1981

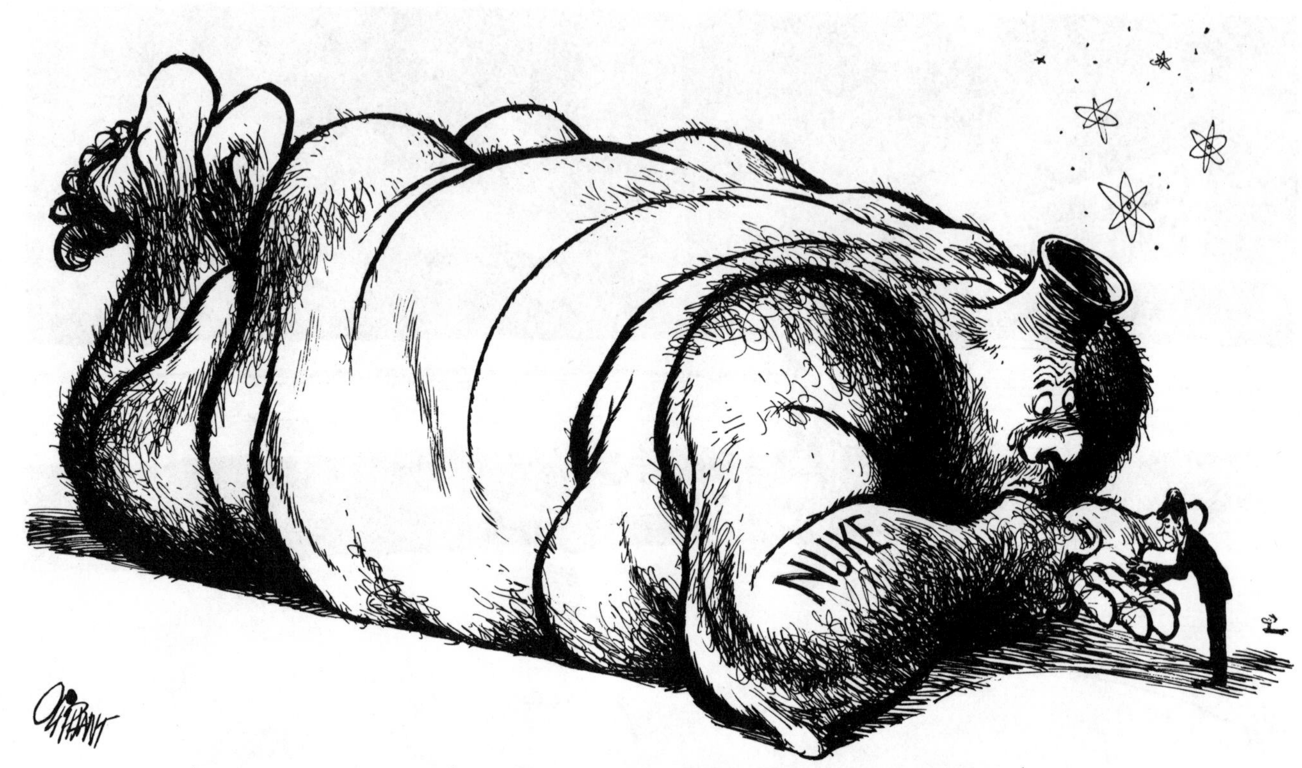

REMOVING THE REGULATORY THORN FROM THE POOR BEAST'S PAW.

October 13, 1981

'GROW INTO IT. DARE TO BE GREAT. KEEP A HIGH PROFILE. KEEP YOUR HEAD DOWN. PURGE THE CRAZIES. BE DEMOCRATIC. TALK TO THE P.L.O.. STICK WITH THE CAMP DAVID ACCORDS...'

October 14, 1981

October 16, 1981

October 19, 1981

'WELL, YES... HE IS A RECESSION. BUT HE'S ONLY A LITTLE ONE.'

October 21, 1981

'WHAT IS BOOTSTRAPS, SENOR?'

October 22, 1981

October 26, 1981

October 28, 1981

'QUICK COLLECTION. CUSTOMER OUT THERE WANTS TO CASH A TWENTY DOLLAR CHECK!'

October 29, 1981

'THIS HERE'S CALLED THE DOOR...'

October 30, 1981

November 2, 1981

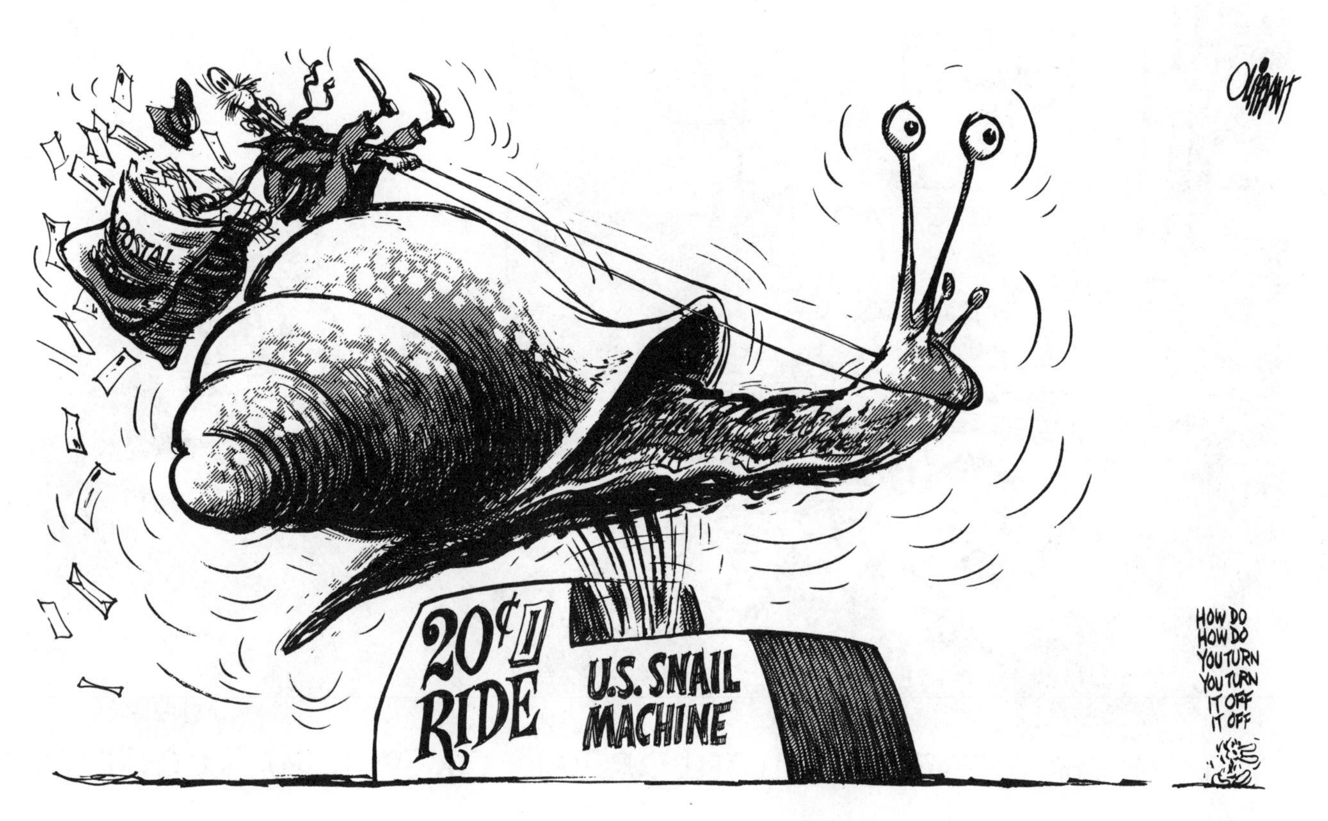

November 3, 1981

'YOU EAT UP YOUR VEGETABLES OR I'LL TELL OUR FAMILY CIA SPY TO PUT YOU ON REPORT.'

November 4, 1981

'STAY DOWN, CHIEF. IT'S ME THEY'RE AFTER. THIS IS GUERRILLA WARFARE, CHIEF. SOMEBODY IS TRYING TO DESTROY AL HAIG. I CAN HANDLE THIS...'

November 6, 1981

November 10, 1981

'BY NAB, I'VE GOT IT! WE'LL GET SOME LONG-TERM CREDIT, WE'LL UPGRADE THE WHOLE PLANT, WE'LL IMPROVE OUR PRODUCTION SCHEDULES, WE'LL HIRE MORE WORKERS, THEY'LL BUY MORE, WE'LL HAVE THE COUNTRY MOVING AGAIN!'

November 11, 1981

'HELLO, LEONID? NO, THERE'S NO NEED TO REPLY. THAT WAS JUST A WARNING SHOT TO KEEP AL HAIG HAPPY!'

November 12, 1981

A VISIT TO THE WOODSHED

November 12, 1981

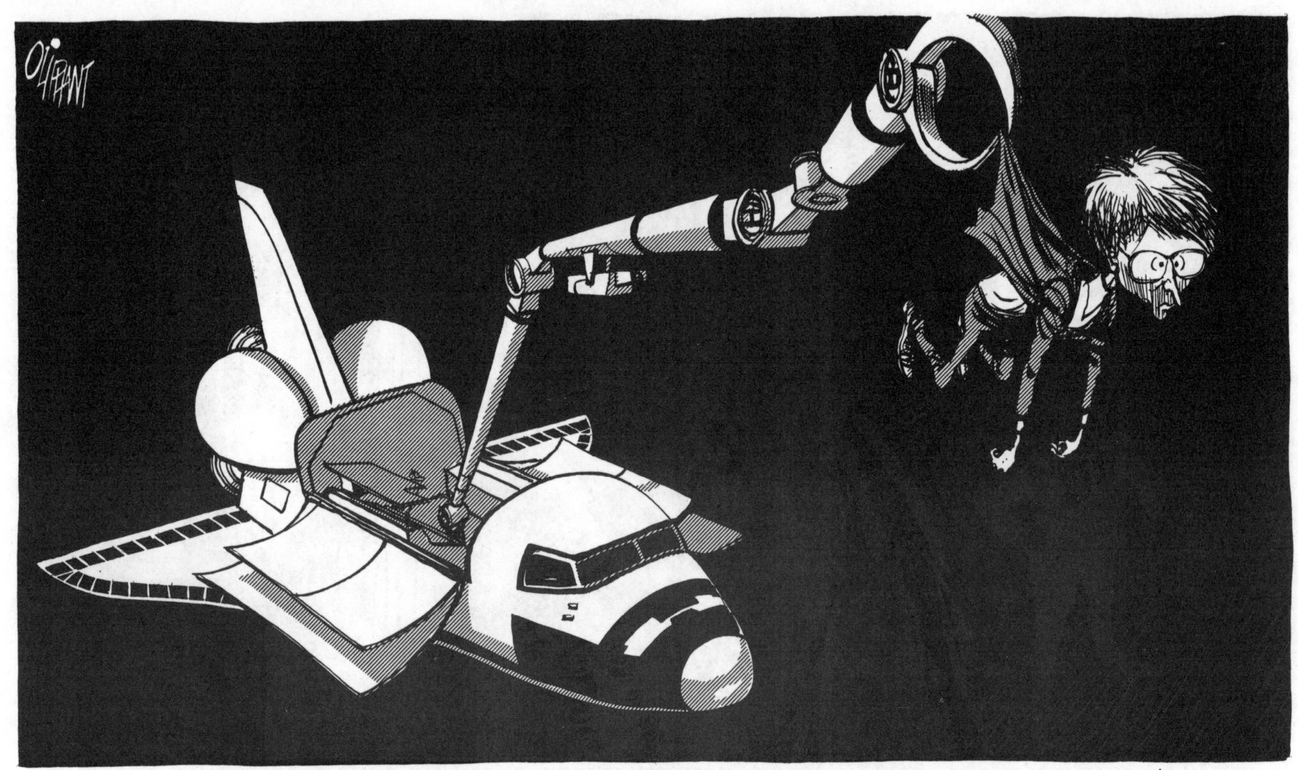

'STOCKMAN RELEASE, TEN SECONDS AND COUNTING... NINE, EIGHT, SEVEN...'

November 16, 1981

November 17, 1981

November 19, 1981

'POOR GUY. ALL THIS LOOSE ARMS-REDUCTION TALK GAVE HIM A NASTY TURN. HEY, GENERAL, IT'S OK — OUR MASSIVE PENTAGON BUDGET IS STILL INTACT.'

November 20, 1981

'SURELY,' SAYS I, 'NOT THE JAMES WATT, FOLK-HERO AND FAMOUS WILDERNESS RAPIST!' 'THAT'S ME,' SAYS HE. AND I SAYS, 'NOT THE RENOWNED DESPOILER OF OUR PRECIOUS NATIONAL HERITAGE!' 'RIGHT,' SAYS HE. SO I ATE HIM.'

November 23, 1981

'PERSONALLY, I'M AGAINST ANY FURTHER CUTTING—WOULDST THOU SETTLE FOR A CONTINUING RESOLUTION UNTIL AFTER THE HOLIDAYS?'

November 24, 1981

November 25, 1981

November 30, 1981

December 1, 1981

December 2, 1981

December 3, 1981

'HOW'S BUSINESS?'

December 4, 1981

December 7, 1981

'LOOK AT US, FELLOW-CREATIONISTS — COULD WE POSSIBLY BE DESCENDED FROM PRIMATES?'

December 9, 1981

December 14, 1981

'THE PARTY SAYS, "EAT!"'

December 16, 1981

December 17, 1981

December 18, 1981

'WHY CAN'T YOU TEACH THE KIDS SOME NICE CREATIONIST SCIENCE, INSTEAD OF THAT EVOLUTIONIST JUNK?'

December 23, 1981

'GIVING HER THAT ELIZABETH TAYLOR DOLL WASN'T SUCH A GREAT IDEA—SHE WOUND IT UP AND IT LEFT.'

December 28, 1981

December 29, 1981

December 30, 1981

January 6, 1982

'BE CONSOLED BY THE FACT THAT THESE HERE AMERICAN-BUILT COMPACTS ARE QUITE A BIT SAFER THAN THE JAPANESE MODELS... THEY SPEND A LOT LESS TIME ON THE HIGHWAY.'

January 7, 1982

'CALIFORNIANS, OF COURSE, LOVE THE RAIN...'

January 11, 1982

January 14, 1982

'BETTER DO AS THEY SAY — SEND OUT THE WEATHERMAN!'

January 14, 1982

'THIS GOVERNMENT OFFICIAL HAS BEEN CLEARED BY THE WHITE HOUSE TO ANSWER ANY QUESTIONS YOU MAY HAVE CONCERNING THE SUPPRESSION OF INFORMATION... IN POLAND.'

January 15, 1982

WRONG-WAY REAGAN

January 18, 1982

January 19, 1982

January 21, 1982

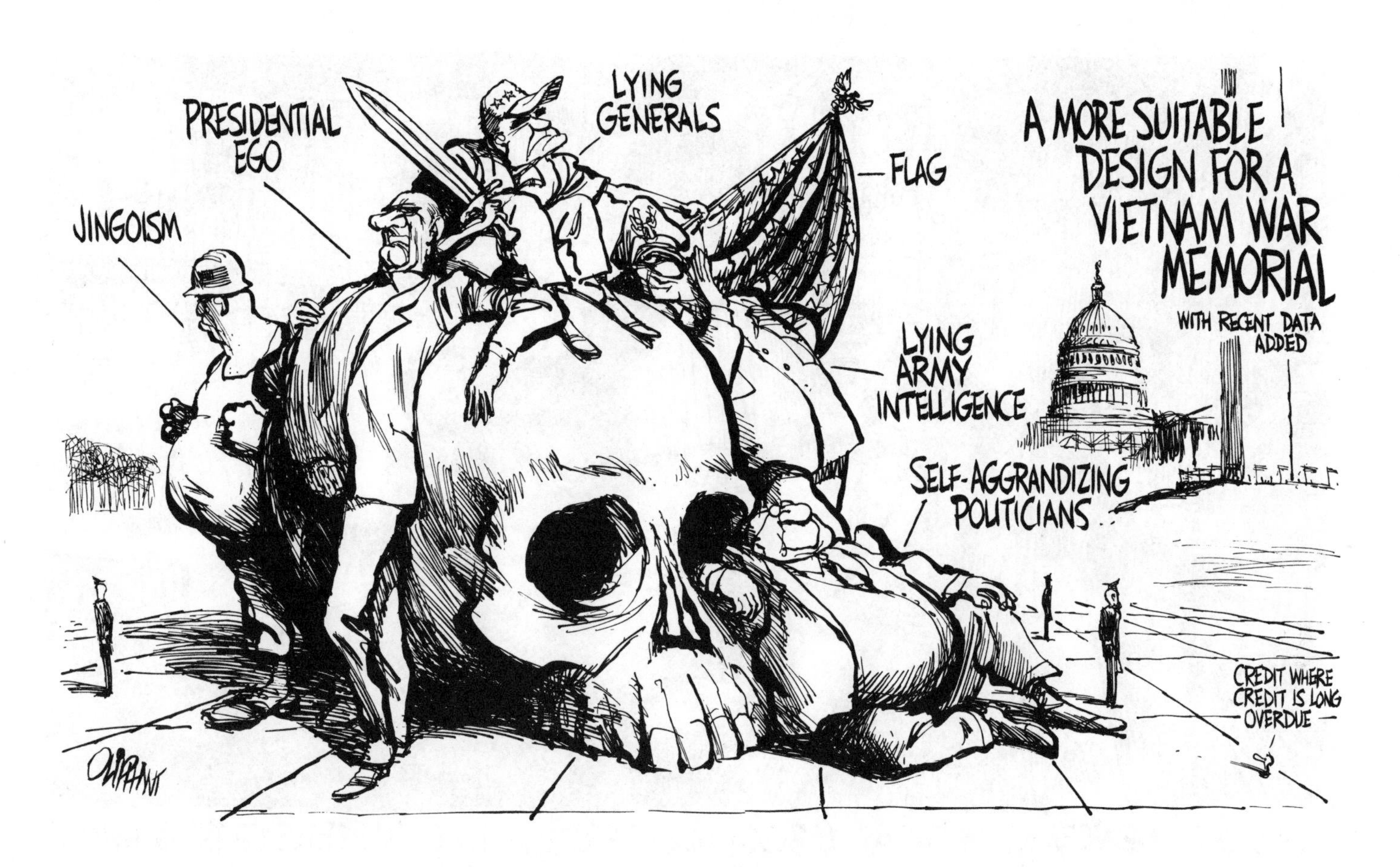

January 25, 1982

'BARTENDER, ONE MORE FOR ME AN' MY OL' BUDDY HERE, BEFORE WE FACE TH' PERILS OF TH' HIGHWAY!'

January 26, 1982

January 29, 1982

'HOW D'YA LIKE THAT? WE USED TO BUILD LEMONS, NOW WE SELL APPLES.'

February 1, 1982

February 2, 1982

'WHY, YOU DEVIL! YOU MEAN YOU JUST DUMP ALL THAT TOXIC WASTE STRAIGHT IN THE RIVER? BUT, ISN'T THAT AWFULLY DANGEROUS?'

February 3, 1982

'THAT'S JUST A SILLY DREAM, HONEY — AIN'T NO BAD OL' BOOGEYMAN UNDER YOUR BED, WAITING TO STEAL YOUR EDUCATION MONEY.'

February 4, 1982

1992 - HISTORIANS REVIEW THE REAGAN TAPES

'THESE ARE OUR OWN TRACKS, SENATOR WEICKER!'

February 10, 1982

'URP! MORE...'

February 11, 1982

February 12, 1982

'THIS ONE IS FOR BEING UNABLE TO FIND WHO MURDERED THE NUNS. THIS ONE IS FOR THE SUDDEN AND AMAZING APPREHENSION OF THE CULPRITS. THIS ONE IS FOR DRAMATIC IMPROVEMENTS IN HUMAN RIGHTS...'

February 16, 1982

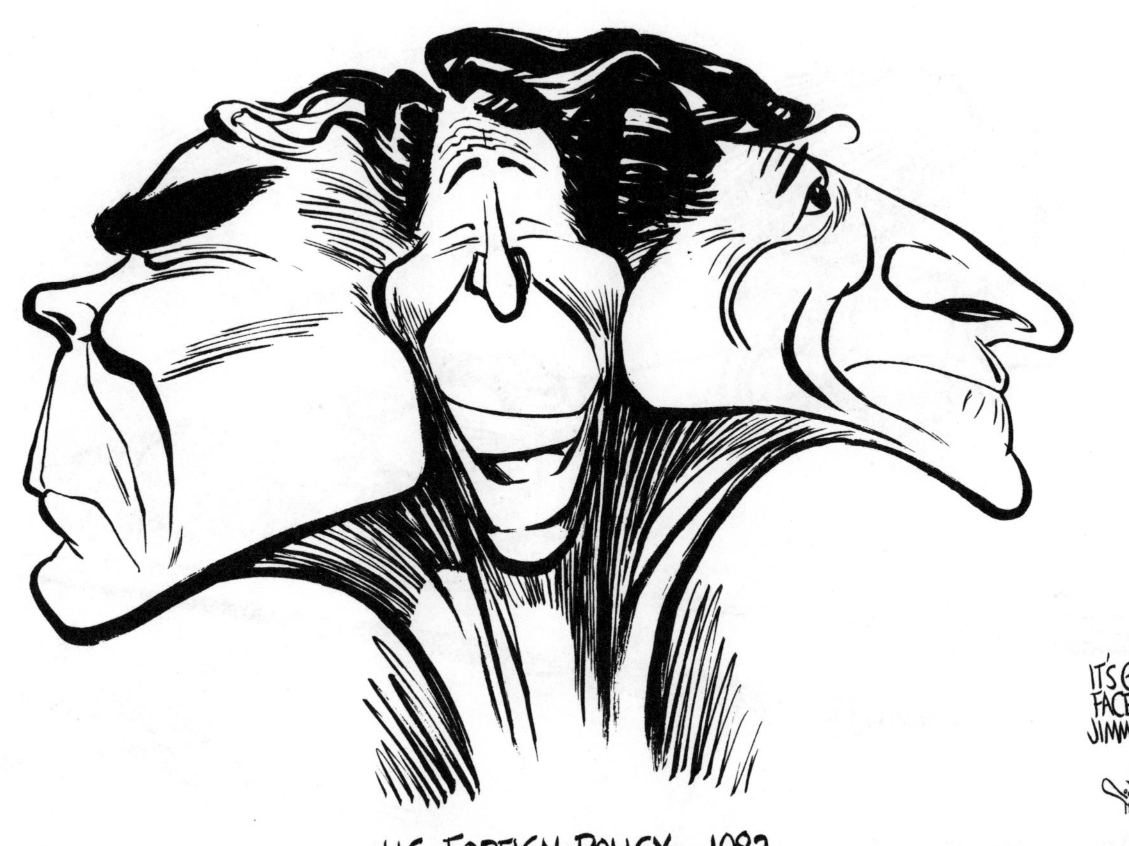

U.S. FOREIGN POLICY—1982

February 18, 1982

THE ADMINISTRATION SAYS IT WILL CONTINUE TO SEND DAVID STOCKMAN TO CAPITOL HILL...

February 19, 1982

THE BEND IN THE TUNNEL

February 22, 1982

'YOU HEARD WATT PROPOSES A BAN ON MINING IN WILDERNESS AREAS?? LET ME SMELL YOUR BREATH!'

February 24, 1982

BUDGET ROUNDUP AT THE DOUBLE-R

February 25, 1982

'SENOR CASTRO EXPORTS HIS REVOLUTION, AND SENOR REAGAN EXPORTS HIS ECONOMIC THEORIES... WHY IS EVERYBODY INTENT ON DESTROYING US?'

February 26, 1982

'MR. BONZO HAS NO COMMENT ON THE CRISIS OTHER THAN TO SAY THAT WITH MR. REAGAN, MR. ASNER AND MR. HESTON INVOLVED, OUR FOREIGN POLICY IS IN THE BEST OF HANDS.'

March 2, 1982

March 4, 1982

I SHOT A DEFICIT INTO THE AIR...
I'LL CHECK YON PEASANT'S BILLFOLD, THERE
BULLSEYE!

March 4, 1982

March 15, 1982

March 17, 1982

'FREEZE!'

March 18, 1982

March 19, 1982

'HI! I'M MAD AS HELL, AND I'M NOT GOING TO TAKE IT ANY MORE!'

March 22, 1982

March 24, 1982

'EASY, SENATOR — IT COULD BE LAWRENCE OF ABSCAM!'

March 25, 1982

March 30, 1982

EYEBALL TO EYEBALL

March 31, 1982

April 1, 1982

OUR COMPLETE ANTI-ENVIRONMENT ARSENAL

April 3, 1982

'WHAT? GIVE AWAY YOUR BIRTHRIGHT TO ARGENTINA? WHY, SON, ONE DAY ALL THIS WILL BE YOURS!'

April 5, 1982

April 6, 1982

ORDER
HOW GOES THE HINCKLEY DEFENSE, COUNSELOR?
WELL, HABEAS CORPII EST ERAT AND ILLEGITIMI NON CARBORUNDUM AGRICOLAE: NOTWITHSTANDING, AND TO WIT IN THE FIRST PART, BUT NOT EXCLUDING THE IMPORTANT WRIT OF INSANIAE AT THE TIMAE. THEN WE HAVE ALL KINDS OF OTHER DODGEII, SHOULD THE AFORESAID GO ABORTIUM...
ORDER ORDER
ORDER ORDER ORDER
VERY GOOD VERY GOOD
QUITE QUITE
JEEZ! IF OSWALD HAD LIVED, THE TRIAL COULD STILL BE PENDING...
WELCOME TO AMERICAN JURISPRUDENCE
RED HERRINGUS
PLEASE WAIT
VERY GOOD FOR THE PROFESSION
QUITE-BUCKS-WISE
OLIPHANT

April 8, 1982

HIPPETY HOPPITY SLIPPETY SLOPPITY— THEY CAN TAKE THIS JOB AND SHOVE IT!
THIS 'SPRING,' LIKEWISE!
OLIPHANT

April 12, 1982

'HOW NICE TO MEET YOU, SEÑOR— I BELIEVE WE HAVE A MUTUAL FRIEND, RONALD REAGAN...'

April 14, 1982

April 15, 1982

'SHE PARAPHRASED YOU PARAPHRASING HER. "FAILURE?' SHE SAID. 'THE POSSIBILITIES DO NOT EXIST."!'

April 16, 1982

'CAN ANYONE TELL ME WHERE THE ENFORCEMENT SECTION IS? HELLO?'

'WHERE ARE YOUR CHANGE-OF-ADDRESS CARDS, PLEASE?'

April 19, 1982

'ARE YOU FINDING IT HARD TO CONCENTRATE?'

April 21, 1982

April 26, 1982

'BLOODY MARVELOUS! WHAT ARE WE SUPPOSED TO DO WITH TWO HUNDRED FLIPPIN' PRISONERS?'

April 28, 1982

April 29, 1982

'IS THERE A DOCTOR OF ECONOMICS IN THE HOUSE?'

April 30, 1982

May 4, 1982

HAW! YOU BIG OIL GUYS ARE TAKING QUITE A BATH THESE DAYS!
OH, MY GOODNESS, YES (SIGH)— HAVE TO ABANDON SYNTHETIC OIL RESEARCH, TAKE HUGE TAX WRITE-OFFS UNTIL THE NEXT SHORTAGE, ETC. (SIGH) ONE WONDERS WHO WILL PAY FOR IT ALL..
GLUT
WAIT! DON'T TELL ME— I USED TO KNOW THAT ANSWER..
OLIPHANT

May 6, 1982

TO OUR GLORIOUS ARGENTINE VICTORY ISLAS MALVINAS 1982
BRITISH TRIUMPH FALKLAND ISLANDS 1982
U.S. SOUTH AMERICAN RELATIONS MAY 1982

May 10, 1982

'LOOK AT IT AS PART OF THE MODIFIED AMERICAN DREAM — OUR FIRST HOUSE IS ALSO A FALL-OUT SHELTER.'

May 11, 1982

'OUT OF THE WAY, YOU COMMIE NUISANCE—ER, NOT YOU, LEONID... THIS OTHER GUY!'

May 12, 1982

ANN LANDERS RE-CYCLES HER COLUMNS. SO DOES DEAR ABBY. AND THE NEW YORK TIMES RE-CYCLES THE CROSSWORD... WHAT ON EARTH IS THE PRESS COMING TO?
EXCUSE ME, MA'AM— WOULD YOU HOLD OUR PLACE IN LINE WHILE MY FRIEND AND I GO FOR COFFEE?
UNEMPLOYMENT OFFICE
UNEMPLOYMENT OFFICE
THINGS ARE WORSE THAN I THOUGHT... EVEN THE POPE IS LAYING THEM OFF!
2-2-75
DEFENSE SPENDING
LAIRD
TAXPAYER
MORE (BURP)
"THE HECK WITH THE DIET!"
6-27-72
ANTI-ANTI-ANTI-ANTI-ANTI-
NTI-ANTI-ANTI MISSILE MISSILE
FASTER!
12-23-66
ARMS LIMITATION TALKS
WHO WAS AHEAD?
". . . HOWEVER, IT'S EXTREMELY IMPORTANT THAT WE KEEP TALKING!"
11-3-70

May 17, 1982

'IF KENNEDY WERE ALIVE, HE WOULD WANT ME PAROLED — THEN I COULD KILL HIM AGAIN!'
OLIPHANT

May 17, 1982

'QUITE FRANKLY, I HAD THOUGHT THE WHOLE BLOODY THING WOULD BE OVER BY NOW!'

May 24, 1982

Y'ALL RECALL ME FROM THE 60s, NO DOUBT...
WHEN I WAS A MEAN, SNARLING, TWO-FISTED, RECALCITRANT, RACIST DEMAGOGUE!
WELL, IN MY NEW CAMPAIGN YOU WILL SEE AH HAVE CHANGED...
NOW, AH AM A KINDLY, SUBDUED, COMPASSIONATE, MORALIST DEMAGOGUE
BUT STILL GOOD OL' GEORGE
OLIPHANT

May 26, 1982

'I DON'T KNOW IF I SHOULD ALSO GO TO BUENOS AIRES... PERHAPS WE SHOULD SEND BILLY GRAHAM.'

May 27, 1982

'HEY, TRUST ME — IF THERE WAS SOMETHING WRONG WITH THESE BEAUTIES, I'D TELL YOU!'

May 28, 1982

USS CANARD
REVISED DESIGN FOR TWO NEW NIMITZ-CLASS AIRCRAFT CARRIERS SOUGHT FOR U.S. NAVY
DOES 'JANE'S' KNOW ABOUT THIS?
OLIPHANT

June 1, 1982

'ER—I THINK HE INTENDS IT TO BE SYMBOLIC OF SOMETHING, MADAM AMBASSADOR—
PERHAPS TO SUGGEST SWEEPING AWAY YOUR MUTUAL DIFFERENCES...OR SOMETHING?...'

June 2, 1982

'...THEN, FROM VERSAILLES TO ROME—OH, MY GOODNESS! THEN, TO ENGLAND TO MEET THE QUEEN, NO LESS! IMAGINE—OUR BOY RIDING WITH THE QUEEN AT WINDSOR! WHAT FUN! THEN, TO BONN...'

'IT IS NOW SEVENTEEN HUNDRED—SAW NO REASON TO WAKE YOU, SO I WENT OVER TO TEN DOWNING STREET TO CHAT TO MAGGIE ON A FEW FOREIGN POLICY MATTERS. THEN, THE QUEEN AND I TOOK A CANTER IN THE PARK...'

June 8, 1982

LONDON PEACE SPEECH
NOW IS THE TIME FOR STATESMAN-LIKE PATIENCE — KICK HIM!

June 9, 1982

'GREAT SHOT, CHAIRMAN ROSTENKOWSKI! YOU WIN A GOLD WATCH, A FREE SET OF CLUBS, AND/OR A FREE TRIP TO PALM SPRINGS!'

June 14, 1982

'INTELLIGENCE IS NOT YET KNOWING WHO IS THIS ANN LANDERS... PERHAPS IS REPLACEMENT FOR JEANE KIRKPATRICK.'

June 15, 1982

ARGENTINA
REAR
ENTRANCE
DON'T CRY FOR ME, ARGENTEEENA
NOT BLOODY LIKELY

June 16, 1982

June 17, 1982

'HEEEY!'

June 18, 1982

'HEY—PSST! WE JUST WANT YOUSE NOT TO WORRY ABOUT MR. DONOVAN — HE'S A GOOD FAMILY MAN!'

June 21, 1982

June 22, 1982

'I THINK I'M GOING NUTS!'

June 23, 1982

'LOOK! THE ROYAL BABY HAS ARRIVED! LET'S ALL TAKE OUR LITTLE FLAGS AND WAVE THEM! NOW, LET'S HAVE THREE CHEERS FOR OUR GOOD FORTUNE...'

June 25, 1982

'THAT TEDDY — ALWAYS THE LIFE OF THE PARTY!'

June 28, 1982

LOOSE CANNON

June 29, 1982

June 30, 1982

July 2, 1982

'O! SAY DOES THAT STAR-SPANGLED BANNER YET WAVE,
O'ER THE LAND OF THE BROKE, WHOSE HOME IS A CAVE?'

July 7, 1982

SURELY, WE IN THE SENATE CAN STAND NO FURTHER SCANDAL!
AS MORAL LEADERS, OUR PERSONAL BEHAVIOUR MUST BE EXEMPLARY!
WHY, OUR LIVES MUST BE AN OPEN BOOK, FIT TO BEAR THE CLOSEST SCRUTINY...
PAGE BY PAGE BY PAGE!
LIKE, CAESAR'S WIFE, HUH?
MORE LIKE, CAESAR'S BOYFRIEND!